Contents

A word from our wonderful sponsors

The Owl Education Institute is an established and unique company. Based in West London we have been offering intensive tuition in the core subjects—English, Mathematics and Science—for over 25 years. The company shamelessly promotes academic, traditional teaching with an emphasis on examination success. We offer high level tutoring in small, focused groups with each teacher head-hunted and selected for his or her individual expertise and brilliance. An excellent centre with an exceptional reputation, we are now proud sponsors of Mr Bruff and look forward to working with him in the year ahead.

Dedication

This guide was written by Georgina Bottomley, part of the mrbruff.com team, and Andrew Bruff.

Georgina Bottomley is an English teacher from Dorset with 14 years of teaching experience. She is a happily married mother of one. Georgina Bottomley would like to thank: Andrew Bruff for his valuable time and expert advice when proofreading the final draft of this book and Neil Bottomley for his on going support.

Andrew and Georgina would also like to thank:

- Sam Perkins, who designed the front cover of this book.
- Sunny Ratilal, who designed the original front cover which was adapted for this edition.

Important note

This guide is not endorsed by, or affiliated with, any exam boards. The writers are simply two experienced English teachers who are using their skills and expertise to help students.

Free gift

Please note: the eBook edition of this guide containtains the complete original text. You deserve that too. Email proof of purchase to info@mrbruff.com and I will send you the eBook edition for free.

Part 1

Introduction

Charles Dickens wrote his novella "A Christmas Carol" in 1843 when he was 31 years old. It is an allegory; Scrooge acts as a symbol for greed and selfishness whilst other characters represent the poor in society and those that are affected by the actions of others who are more fortunate.

Today, over 170 years later, the story continues to be read and studied across the world. So what is it about this tale that keeps generation after generation so intrigued? Why has it been retold so many times? Even the Muppets have starred in a film version of this story!

In this eBook we shall look for the lessons of social responsibility that Dickens is trying to teach the reader. Along the way we will analyse language, structure, form, character, theme, context and much more; hopefully you will find it useful.

If you consider this revision guide valuable then please visit and subscribe to my YouTube Channel (youtube.com/mrbruff) where you will find hundreds of videos focusing on English and English Literature. The videos have been viewed over 11 million times across 198 nations – we'd love you to join in.

A number of other printed Mr Bruff titles, including the bestselling revision guide for GCSE English and English Literature, can be bought via Amazon.

Andrew Bruff

April 2017

Part 2

The Author - Charles Dickens

Charles Dickens was born in Hampshire, England in 1812, He had an education which was interrupted by moving around and at one point Dickens was even sent to work in a blacking factory aged only 11. He lived in poverty as his father had been jailed for his inability to pay his debts. His views on poverty and the treatment of the poor are very clear in this novella and in many of his other works. Despite his difficult childhood, Dickens did return to education and later wrote about some of these experiences in his novels such as "Great Expectations" and "David Copperfield." His many journeys around London, no doubt, add to his ability to describe the city in such a vivid way.

After leaving school Dickens worked for a solicitor and then later as a journalist, writing for a variety of publications. He had his first short story published in 1833 when he was 21. He went on to write in a variety of different forms including weekly periodicals, plays, travel books, novels and an autobiography.

Charles Dickens married Catherine Hogarth in 1836. By this point he had become a popular author thanks to the "Pickwick Papers" and novels such as "Oliver Twist" and "Nicholas Nickleby."

In 1842 he visited America and briefly lost his popularity but the publication of "A Christmas Carol" in 1843 soon restored his reputation as a great writer. The novella was very well received by readers and critics alike.

Dickens continued to travel and write. He began to give public readings of his works in 1858, the same year he separated from his wife Catherine.

Still in the middle of writing "The Mystery of Edwin Drood," Charles Dickens died in June 1870, aged 58. He is buried in Westminster Abbey in London, England. His intentions for the ending of "The Mystery of Edwin Drood" remain unknown.

How are Dickens's beliefs reflected in "A Christmas Carol"?

Dickens truly believed that there shouldn't be so much of a divide between people who are rich and those who are less well off. The novella focuses on the problems faced by poor people and their behaviour and attitudes, in contrast to the rich. Dickens seems to be trying to make readers consider whether or not they are supportive to others and able to take responsibility for their actions towards their family members and the rest of the local community. He is very critical of rich businessmen who he believed exploited the poor for their own gains.

Dickens was also concerned with the treatment of children. In Dickens's time many children were put to work in factories and other businesses which required hard labour, many from a very early age. Through his work Dickens criticises this treatment of children and the poor and suggests that those who were well-off were likely to appear uncaring about such issues. He attempts to highlight the problems to readers and suggest a change for the future.

Is 'A Christmas Carol' still relevant today?

Whilst times have, thankfully, changed and Britain no longer sees children used purely for their hard labour, the case is sadly not the same across the rest of the world. The novella may therefore still be seen as important to highlight those issues for modern readers.

In addition, the conditions and pay of workers can still be seen as important issues today. In 'A Christmas Carol' we see Bob Cratchit struggling to support his family despite working hard for Scrooge. Although life is clearly hard for them, the Cratchit family still manage to make the best of their situation and enjoy celebrating Christmas together. This message, about making the best of your situation and appreciating time with your family, will almost certainly resonate with any reader. The exploitation of workers could also be seen as relevant as many people are arguably not paid a fair wage both in our society and in other communities across the world.

The idea of social responsibility is an enduring message which must be seen as valuable to any reader. No matter your social status or hardships, remaining honest, friendly and fair to others is surely crucial to a happy future society.

Part 3

Structure

Understanding the title

It is slightly strange that a novella should be called a "carol." As we all know, carols are songs sung at Christmas; they usually have a Christian feel to them and often use rhyme and rhythm to make the lyrics memorable. Certainly the novella does have many religious connotations which are discussed further in the section about the story being an allegory.

Interestingly, Dickens uses prose which neither rhymes nor is rhythmical. He may, however, hope that the story is re-told or listened to repeatedly… after all, storytelling has been a tradition for many hundreds of years. If that was indeed the case Dickens has certainly had his wish come true as "A Christmas Carol" has been re-told many times in many different ways. There are several feature films of the story and now that it is one of the possible set texts for G.C.SE English Literature, no doubt even more will become familiar with the narrative.

Another oddity about the story is that it contains ghosts. It is fairly rare for a Christmas story to contain ghosts, they are more likely to have references to elves, reindeer and Father Christmas!

It might be these original features which mean "A Christmas Carol" stands out among many Christmas tales.

What is a novella?

"A Christmas Carol" is written in the form of a novella. A novella is traditionally longer than a short story, but not as long as a traditional novel. Novellas often have some sort of moral or lesson which the writer is trying to teach the reader, consequently there is often a protagonist whom learns this same lesson.

"A Christmas Carol" is presented in this way as it focuses on the main character, Ebenezer Scroooge, learning the benefits of being a responsible citizen and caring for his family and other members of society. Dickens may have been responding to a need at the time for a short text which was relatively easily to follow. It could be seen as ideal reading for the Christmas period!

What is a stave?

Rather than chapters, "A Christmas Carol" is divided into five "staves." Staves are generally used in songs. It can be seen as another name for a verse.

The use of the word "stave" may relate to the title, with it being a "Carol" or Christmas song. Dickens was a fan of music, particularly classical pieces by composers such as Mozart and he even wrote some songs himself so that may have further influenced his choice of term. A stave of music has five lines so it is therefore somewhat unsurprising that Dickens includes five staves in "A Christmas Carol."

It might also be argued that the use of "staves" emphasises the relatively short nature of each of the 5 sections and gives a light-hearted feel to the story. Dickens further emphasises this in the Preface when he says that his intention was to write a book which "shall not put my readers out of humour with themselves."

Structure of the story

In many ways "A Christmas Carol" is a story of time-travel. The moving around from the present to the past, back to the present and into the future, before returning to the present could be very confusing, but Marley's visit explains that there will be three more spirits for Scrooge to learn from, "You will be haunted… by Three Spirits." Marley's visit makes the upcoming structure clear. Since both the reader and Scrooge know what to expect, it is a relatively easy structure to follow.

In order that Scrooge can return to Christmas Day, time is played with, by Dickens. The spirits all visit Scrooge at 1am; he goes to sleep at 2am, then wakes up at midnight again, so time seems to somehow re-set itself. Without the action all happening in one single night, Scrooge would wake up after Christmas Day is over and would be less able to put his new caring attitude into practice.

Dickens seems to blur the boundaries between appearance and reality and we, the readers, are required to suspend our disbelief, so that the message Dickens is delivering about the need to take responsibility for each other, can be understood. The climax of the novella, when Scrooge sees his own name on a gravestone and finally not only accepts he must change his ways but is keen to do so, is followed by a resolution where we see Scrooge putting his words into action. He shows that he is now willing to look out for other people and accept his responsibilities towards his family and employees.

What is an allegory?

The novella can be seen as a Christian story of redemption. Scrooge can be viewed as representative of the wealthy and aristocratic members of society at the time. Through him, Dickens argues that those with money are often uncaring towards those with less money than themselves. Their demeanour is presented as selfish and they seem to focus on making more money rather than looking out for the welfare of others, including their employees.

Fred Scrooge and Fezziwig represent the middle class who are more generous and keen to prioritise others rather than themselves, particularly at Christmas. Both throw parties for their family and friends; Fezziwig also includes his employees showing that businessmen don't have to be heartless and uncaring as Scrooge has been. Fred effectively acts as a contrast or "foil" to Scrooge, demonstrating that it is rewarding to spend money on Christmas festivities and it is possible to be determined and focused without being neglectful. Fred insists he will continue to invite Scrooge to his house every Christmas no matter how many times his invitation is turned down by the old miser!

Ignorance and Want are two characters presented by the Ghost of Christmas Present. They are said to be the children of mankind. Scrooge is warned to fear Ignorance more than Want, "This boy is Ignorance. This girl is Want. Beware them both, and all of their degree; but most of all beware the boy, for on his brow I see that written which is Doom…" Ignorance represents members of society who are uneducated and maybe unaware that they are being exploited as workers. Dickens argues that if children are educated, then they are more likely to be able to earn a fair wage and support their families.

The message of social responsibility is repeated to Scrooge throughout the novel, right from Marley's visit early in the story. The message is therefore impossible for the reader to ignore too!

Part 4

Context - A Victorian Christmas

Many believe that the nature of our Christmas celebrations in Britain dates back to the 1840s when Prince Albert married Queen Victoria. The decorated Christmas tree is thought to have been brought to Britain from Germany by Albert in 1841; it was soon adopted by most homes who wanted to join in the festivities. The Christmas card dates back to 1843 when Henry Cole asked an artist to design one for him. They were expensive, at one shilling each, so many children began making their own and sending those. Eventually the idea of sending cards grew and of course many of us still send cards today. Even serving turkey as the main meat at Christmas comes from the Victorians. They also enjoyed singing carols, the first collection being published in 1833.

Like most Victorians, Dickens enjoyed spending Christmas with his family. They would eat well, play games and enjoy each other's company. The novella is said to help to broadcast the message of the traditions of Christmas. Dickens believed it should be a time of peace and goodwill to everyone, no matter their social status. That Christmas spirit is still spread by many today with some people choosing to spend some of their holidays helping others and ensuring they are supported and cared for. There are of course, some who adopt a more "Bah Humbug!" approach to the festivities so hopefully Scrooge's story will continue to be enjoyed and its message talked about for many years to come!

Context - Poverty in Victorian Britain

Dickens was acutely aware of the poverty that was evident in Victorian Britain. Lots of people were living in cramped conditions as cities became overpopulated due to the Industrial Revolution. These conditions meant that crime was difficult to control and disease was rife due to the poor, unsanitary living conditions. Sewers struggled to cope with the increased demand.

Many worked long hours in factories whereas prior to the Industrial Revolution, more worked the land as farmers. It was a time when rich businessmen and owners of the factories exploited their workers, expecting them to work extremely long hours for very little pay.

Dickens himself experienced poverty when his family went into debt when he was still a child. Several of his works include reference to poverty including "Little Dorrit", "Hard Times" and of course, "A Christmas Carol."

In the novella we see Scrooge (a representative of hard-hearted businessmen) contrasted with the poor but hard working Cratchit family. See the chapters about these characters and the essay about wealth and poverty for further analysis.

In 1834 the New Poor Law was introduced to Britain to try and combat the large numbers of poor people in the country at the time. It stated that in order to receive any financial assistance anyone without a job was required to enter a workhouse if they wished to receive support with money and housing. There was a belief that poor people were lazy, so workhouses were deliberately very difficult places (Dickens likens them to prisons) to discourage people from wanting to go there.

Dickens was against this new law and he has criticised it in some of his other works such as Oliver Twist and his later journals.

In "A Christmas Carol" it is the men who are collecting money at the start of the novella that make the situation clear, "Many thousands are in want of common necessities." Dickens also presents education as a way out of poverty through his use of the two children Ignorance and Want. See the chapters on those characters for further analysis.

Part 5

Summary of the story

Preface: I have endeavoured in this Ghostly little book, to raise the Ghost of an Idea, which shall not put my readers out of humour with themselves, with each other, with the season, or with me. May it haunt their houses pleasantly, and no one wish to lay it.

Their faithful Friend and Servant, C.D.

December, 1843.

In this Preface Dickens sets out his intentions – to write a short book which includes ghosts but not those which will terrify the reader. The book will not cause readers to be upset with themselves, others, Christmas or Dickens himself. He hopes the book will be enjoyed.

The introduction – Scrooge is a selfish miser who hates Christmas!

Ebenezer Scrooge is the protagonist in Dickens's 'A Christmas Carol.' He is a lonely miser who is most concerned with his money and, to be frank, himself. As the novella begins we learn that Scrooge's business partner Jacob Marley has died, leaving Scrooge alone at work in his office in London save for his clerk, Bob Cratchit. The novella starts on Christmas Eve; Scrooge appears irritated that Christmas appears to be interrupting his business and he is very reluctant to give Bob Cratchit Christmas Day off work.

Scrooge's irritation continues as he refuses his nephew Fred's invitation to join his family for Christmas dinner, "every idiot who goes about with 'Merry Christmas' on his lips, should be boiled in his own pudding, and buried with a stake of holly through his heart." He also refuses to donate any money when two gentlemen call to collect money for the poor. Scrooge is presented as a selfish man who has no sympathy for those less fortunate than himself.

As he returns home that evening, Scrooge is shocked when his door knocker momentarily seems to transform into the face of Jacob Marley (Scrooge's former business partner who has been dead for seven years.) This foreshadows the arrival of the ghost of Jacob Marley later that night.

Jacob Marley's Visit – Scrooge is warned he must change his ways

Tensions are raised as Scrooge hears bells and chains which signal the arrival of Marley's ghost. When Marley was alive he and Scrooge became known for their ruthless methods; they were unloved loan sharks who cared little for others and exploited other people's misfortune to make money. Marley is now seen bound in chains as if he is being punished for his poor behaviour and lack of responsibility for others whilst he was alive. Marley warns Scrooge that he, too, will suffer for his actions if he does not change his cold-hearted ways. "It is required of every man... that the spirit within him should walk abroad among his fellow-men, and travel far and wide; and if that spirit goes not forth in life, it is condemned to do so after death." Marley then sets up the structure of the next section of the novella as he explains that Scrooge will be visited by three more ghosts…

The Ghost of Christmas Past – reminds Scrooge of his happy childhood

Later that same night (around 1am) the first ghost visits Ebenezer Scrooge. This spirit takes the appearance of both a child and an old man and has a light which makes him look somewhat like a candle. He tells Scrooge that he is the Ghost of Christmas Past. He takes Scrooge to the place he grew up. Scrooge is reminded how his friends would go home for Christmas while he was left at school. Readers may begin to feel some sympathy for Scrooge at this point.

Next the ghost reminds Scrooge of when his sister Fan (Fred's mother) took him home from school for Christmas one year. He is then whisked to a party thrown by Fezziwig, Scrooge's boss to whom he was an apprentice when he was a young man.

Finally the spirit shows Scrooge the Christmas when his fiancée, Belle, decided that she didn't want to be with someone as selfish and driven by money as Scrooge. He is forced to see her happily married to someone else and with a family of her own. Belle's husband even comments how he had seen Scrooge working alone. Scrooge forces the ghost to leave by hitting him over the head with a candle extinguisher! He then falls back to sleep.

The Ghost of Christmas Present – shows Scrooge how others celebrate Christmas

The next night when Scrooge is woken at 1am he finds his home has magically been decorated for Christmas. There is a feast laid out and a fire roars in the hearth.

The Ghost of Christmas Present looks somewhat like Father Christmas as he is dressed in long, green robes. He takes Scrooge on a tour of the houses of the local residents. Here Scrooge sees that despite poverty, his neighbours are celebrating and enjoying Christmas; they are making the best of what they have.

The spirit takes Scrooge to visit the house belonging to Bob Cratchit and his family. Scrooge clearly doesn't pay his clerk very much but despite this Bob, Mrs. Cratchit and their children are enjoying a small Christmas dinner. We meet Tiny Tim, Bob's son who is crippled and very ill. The ghost informs Scrooge that the child will die soon if his situation does not improve. Scrooge listens to the family's conversation and hears Mrs. Cratchit's criticism of him.

The ghost then takes Scrooge to other households, all of whom are celebrating Christmas in their own way. Finally he is taken to his nephew Fred's house. He had earlier refused to join Fred and his family for Christmas dinner. Again he finds he is being talked about. As he listens to the conversation he learns that Fred is still hopeful that Scrooge will join them one day. His persistence and hope is to be applauded.

Despite his earlier reservations Scrooge can't help but join in the party games, even though he isn't visible to the rest of the family. Before he can get too carried away though, the Ghost of Christmas Present shows Scrooge two children whom he calls Ignorance and Want. "This boy is Ignorance. This girl is Want. Beware them both, and all of their degree; but most of all beware the boy, for on his brow I see that written which is Doom…" Here Dickens seems to suggest that Want (or need) is to be feared but that Ignorance is the worst trait as that can lead to Want. If people are educated and taught how to work and provide for their families and how to look out for one another then the cycle of poverty can be broken and avoided in the future. If the poor remain uneducated then they cannot improve their situations.

The Ghost of Christmas Yet to Come – shows Scrooge how he will die a lonely and unhappy man unless he changes his ways

The final ghost to appear to Scrooge arrives dressed in a long black cloak, not dissimilar to that worn by the Grim Reaper. He has Scrooge listen to a conversation about a man's death, although Scrooge has no idea at this time that the dead man they are discussing is actually himself! It is clear that nobody cares about the man's death.

Next, Scrooge sees people selling items which have been stolen from the dead man's house. The spirit the takes Scrooge back to Bob Cratchit's house. The Cratchit family are grieving for Tiny Tim who has now died. Scrooge wants to know who the dead man is so the ghost, before he vanishes, takes him to view a grave. The grave belongs to Ebenezer Scrooge himself.

The Ending – Scrooge is a changed man

Following the final ghost's visit, Scrooge realises that he must change his miserly ways. He sends a massive turkey to Bob Cratchit and his family and he gives Bob a raise. Scrooge also makes a donation to help the poor (which he refused to do when the portly gentlemen had visited him on Christmas Eve) and decides to attend Christmas dinner at Fred's house.

Scrooge looks out for Tiny Tim (who is alive) and it seems he is now going to be remembered as someone who is more than capable of looking out for others, and celebrating Christmas of course!

Check your understanding

A quick quiz, based on the summary you've just read

1. Who was Scrooge's business partner who later visits him as a ghost?

2. Who is Scrooge's clerk?

3. Before he returns home Scrooge declines two invitations, what are they?

4. Which inanimate object turns into the face of Jacob Marley?

5. Which sounds signal the arrival of Marley's ghost?

6. Why is Marley being punished in the afterlife?

7. Where does the Ghost of Christmas Past take Scrooge?

8. What do we learn about Bob Cratchit's family Christmas thanks to the Ghost of Christmas Present?

9. Which does the Ghost of Christmas Present tell Scrooge to fear the most: Ignorance or Want?

10. What is the Ghost of Christmas Yet to Come dressed in?

11. What is happening to Scrooge's belongings now that he's died?

12. What is the final sight that makes Scrooge determined to change his ways?

13. When the spirits have left and Scrooge is returned to the present, what does he send to the Cratchit family?

14. Which invitations does Scrooge now accept that he refused at the start of the story?

15. What lesson has Scrooge learned by the end of the novella?

Part 6

Analysis of the Characters

Ebenezer Scrooge

(see the sample essay exploring his transformation for more detailed analysis of this character)

Ebenezer Scrooge is the protagonist of the novella. We follow his journey from a miserable penny-pincher to a man who realises the error of his ways and transforms into a more caring and compassionate citizen. Dickens uses Scrooge to criticise the divide between those who have money and those who do not.

Scrooge is a lonely character at the start of the novella. Dickens's use of language reflects this when outlining Scrooge's relationship with his former clerk Marley, "Scrooge was the sole executor, his sole administrator, his sole assign, his sole residuary legatee, his sole friend, and sole mourner." The repetition of the word "sole" adds emphasis to the solitary nature of the lives led by Marley and now Scrooge. Dickens sums him up as, "a squeezing, wrenching, grasping, scraping, clutching, covetous old sinner!" The collection of verbs here define Scrooge as a character whose intention is to grab every last penny he can from anyone he encounters.

Scrooge is described as "hard and sharp as flint," Thanks to this simile he seems to have a hard exterior which could cause pain to others. Similarly, Scrooge is described as, "solitary as an oyster." This simile, unlike the first, does suggest that there may be more to be discovered where Scrooge is concerned. Just as, when forced open, an oyster may contain a pearl so Dickens suggests there may be something worthwhile to be found within Scrooge too. There is also a literal and metaphorical coldness associated with the early descriptions of Scrooge, "A frosty rime was on his head, and on his eyebrows, and his wiry chin. He carried his own low temperature always about with him…" Dickens's use of language again emphasises Scrooge's cold-hearted nature and attitude towards others.

Scrooge rejects his nephew Fred's best wishes with a "Bah! Humbug!" refuses to give any money to the two gentleman who are collecting for the poor and resists giving his clerk Bob Cratchit any time off for Christmas, "It's not convenient."

When faced with Marley's ghost we finally see a more vulnerable side to Scrooge. He implores the ghost to help him, despite having resisted opportunities to help others earlier in the day, "Speak comfort to me, Jacob." He has a taste of his own medicine when the ghost replies, "I have none to give." From early in the novella Dickens makes it clear that we reap what we sow in life and in order for people to care about us we must care for them and look out for them in return.

The Ghost of Christmas Past seems to care for Scrooge and Scrooge returns to an almost childlike state in his presence. When visiting his old school the ghost describes how Scrooge "A solitary child, neglected by his friends, is left there still." At this Scrooge shows some emotion and cries. He is similarly moved when reminded of his sister, his former employer Fezziwig and his love, Belle who broke up with him due to his obsession with money. It is apparent Scrooge is starting to realise that it is not only money which brings happiness.

Before the ghost leaves, Scrooge again makes it clear he is reflecting on his recent behaviour towards Bob Cratchit, "I should like to be able to say a word or two to my clerk just now!"

When the Ghost of Christmas Present appears, we are reminded that Scrooge's attitude is changing, "I went forth last night on compulsion, and I learnt a lesson which is working now. To-night, if you have aught to teach me, let me profit by it." He is prepared for the lessons which await him.

Scrooge is taken by the Ghost of Christmas Present and shown people celebrating Christmas, including the Cratchit household. Scrooge sees Tiny Tim struggling and sees how the family are able to celebrate despite not having much money. Scrooge implores the ghost to tell him of the future, "tell me if Tiny Tim will live." He genuinely seems to care about the little boy's fate, in contrast to his early comments about the poor and how if they die it would "decrease the surplus population." His attitude is certainly changing.

When visiting the house of his nephew Fred, Scrooge is again made to watch those appearing in the vision enjoying the festivities without him. He enjoys the party and "begged like a boy to stay." There is now hope for Scrooge's future as it is not too late for him to rejoin his family and celebrate Christmas for the first time in many years.

No sooner does the Ghost of Christmas Present disappear, than the final spirit, the Ghost of Christmas Yet to Come takes his place. The shrouded figure appears as a personification of Death to warn Scrooge that he is facing a lonely end and further torment if he does not start thinking of others and caring for those around him.

Initially, this spirit shows Scrooge a group of people who are talking about a man's death, "It's likely to be a very cheap funeral, for upon my life I don't know of anybody to go to it." At first Scrooge cannot work out which person has died. He is then taken to a group who are sorting through his belongings. The group again talk about the dead man in a very negative way, calling him "a wicked old screw." They have even stolen the blanket Scrooge was due to be buried in, in a similarly uncaring way to the way Scrooge has been acting towards others.

Scrooge does eventually realise that this is the aftermath of his own death that he's witnessing, "I see. The case of this unhappy man might be my own." After visiting a family who are pleased Scrooge has died because it meant they might have some relief from their debts, and the Cratchits who are mourning the death of Tiny Tim, the spirit takes Scrooge to a churchyard. It is here that Scrooge reads his own name on a gravestone and realises the sad future that lies in wait for him if he refuses to change his ways. He vows to "honour Christmas in my heart, and try to keep it all the year. I will live in the Past, the Present, and the Future. The Spirits of all Three shall strive within me. I will not shut out the lessons that they teach." At this point the ghost disappears and Scrooge is returned to bed.

In the final section of the novella, Scrooge describes himself using figurative language, "I am as light as a feather, I am as happy as an angel, I am as merry as a school-boy..." He even laughs, "it was a splendid laugh, a most illustrious laugh. The father of a long, long line of brilliant laughs!"

Scrooge arranges for a big turkey to be sent to the Cratchits, wishes others a "Merry Christmas" then goes to Fred's house for a "Wonderful party." Already Scrooge is reaping the rewards of making an effort and being friendly to others.

At the office the next morning Scrooge gives Bob Cratchit a rise in wages. The final paragraphs of the novella confirm that Scrooge is indeed a changed man, "Scrooge was better than his word. He did it all and infinitely more." His journey is complete and we, the readers, are left with the understanding that people can change and society is a better place if we all look out for one another.

Fred Scrooge

Fred is Scrooge's nephew. He is the son of Fan, Scrooge's sister and is Scrooge's only relative who is still alive. He can be seen as the opposite of Scrooge in many ways. He appears to symbolise the good in people and shows the reader how we should behave towards one another.

We first meet Fred when he arrives to wish Scrooge a Merry Christmas, "A merry Christmas, uncle! God save you!" It is the response to this greeting that is one of Dickens's most well-known lines, "'Bah!' said Scrooge, 'Humbug!'"

Whereas Scrooge is likened to frost and ice, "his thin lips blue... a frosty rime was on his head," so Fred is compared to warmth and heat, "He had so heated himself with rapid walking... his face was all in a glow." Fred emits both a physical and metaphorical warmth to those around him.

Even though Scrooge hasn't made any time for his family, Fred still persists and does what is right; he visits his Uncle and delivers the season's greetings. Unlike Scrooge who hates Christmas, Fred sees it as a "kind, forgiving, charitable, pleasant time." In this way we are aware that Scrooge's isolation is through his own choice and free will - it hasn't been imposed on him by members of his family.

When Scrooge is a boy, Fan collects him from school and shows him similar affection to that which Fred shows him in the present. This shows there was potential for Scrooge to have positive, loving relationships with his family but so far he has chosen a more selfish path.

At his own Christmas party Fred refuses to be heavily critical of Scrooge's self-centered ways when maybe he is entitled to be. He is determined to welcome Scrooge back into the family if he's ever given the opportunity, "I mean to give him the same chance every year, whether he likes it or not, for I pity him." Fred might be entitled to be somewhat irritated with Scrooge's repeated rejections but he almost appears stubborn in his refusal to give up on his Uncle.

Fred is kind and friendly to others he meets and at the end of the novella, welcomes Scrooge back into the family, "Let him in!" despite the way Scrooge has been treating him. His unfailing way of accepting flaws and remaining friendly despite the circumstances, arguably makes Fred somewhat unbelievable as a character. He can certainly be seen as a symbol of good; he is used by Dickens as a role model to the reader, showing us how we should behave. He can serve as an effective comparison to Scrooge in a range of exam answers.

Check your understanding

Scrooge and Fred – A Comparison:

Fill in the grid to show the similarities and differences between the two characters. Check your answers at the end of the book:

Scrooge	Fred

The Cratchit Family

Bob Cratchit is Scrooge's clerk. He and his family arguably represent the poor and needy in society. Despite struggling for money, Bob is a reliable, loving and kind man who makes the best of his situation, "They were not a handsome family; they were not well dressed; their shoes were far from being water-proof; their clothes were scanty… But, they were happy, grateful, pleased with one another, and contented with the time."

Bob is a dedicated employee of Scrooge's, even though Scrooge treats him badly. At the start of the novella we see how he is unable to even keep himself warm at work, "Scrooge had a very small fire, but the clerk's fire was so very much smaller that it looked like one coal. But he couldn't replenish it, for Scrooge kept the coal-box in his own room."

It could be argued that the Cratchits seem so perfect that it is somewhat difficult to see them as real people.

Bob Cratchit is a caring father. Tiny Tim is his youngest son and one of the most well-known characters in the story. He is a cripple who is on the verge of death, although the exact nature of his affliction is unclear and therefore leaves the reader in some suspense as to whether or not he is likely to survive. Despite his difficulties, Tim and his family have kept their faith, "He hoped the people saw him in the church, because he was a cripple, and it might be pleasant to them to remember upon Christmas Day, who made lame beggars walk, and blind men see." At the end of the novella Tiny Tim's condition improves drastically thanks to money that has been given to the family by Scrooge. Again this situation could be criticised as being too perfect and therefore somewhat unbelievable as a character. Tim might better be seen as a symbol of the consequences of Scrooge's change in attitude and behaviour in the story. After all, we are all required to suspend our disbelief anyway thanks to the use of time-travelling ghosts in a Christmas story!

Peter Cratchit is Bob Cratchit's eldest son, Martha Cratchit is his oldest daughter and Mrs. Cratchit is Bob Cratchit's wife. Mrs. Cratchit makes an effort with her appearance even though the family have very little money, "dressed out but poorly in a twice-turned gown, but brave in ribbons, which are cheap and make a goodly show for sixpence." She is very caring towards her family and does not really agree with her husband that they should be thankful towards Scrooge for what little money they have. Bob Cratchit toasts his boss as the "Founder of the Feast" but Mrs. Cratchit is reluctant to join him in giving thanks in this way. She dislikes Scrooge because she sees how hard her husband works for him and yet is not really rewarded for his efforts or even treated fairly. Mrs. Cratchit shows that some women at the time were starting to voice their own opinions and stand up for their beliefs, even though the suffragette movement was yet to emerge.

The foreshadowing of Tiny Tim's death is one of the ways in which Scrooge is forced to realise he must change his selfish ways and start paying Bob fairly.

Fan

Fan Scrooge is Fred's mother and Scrooge's sister. During his visit to his childhood with the Ghost of Christmas Past, Scrooge appears happy as he is greeted by Fan from school and taken home. She "stood on tiptoe to embrace him. Then she began to drag him, in her childish eagerness, towards the door." Scrooge's interactions with Fan show that he did enjoy the company of his family at one point in his life and it has been his choice to distance himself from them as he has grown up. Fan had one child, his nephew Fred but she later died. Unanswered questions remain about her death so the reader is left to fill in the gaps. Some readers may find the gaps in the story intriguing, other may feel some frustration at the lack of clarity. What are your thoughts?

Fezziwig

Scrooge worked for Fezziwig when he was a young man in London. The Ghost of Christmas Past takes Scrooge on another trip down memory lane to a time when he was apprenticed to the jolly businessman.

Fezziwig is proof that a man can make money and yet still be a fair employer and a happy individual. We see him dancing with his wife and celebrating at their Christmas party. Dickens is suggesting that it is possible to be successful in business and share the wealth to an extent that others may be happy. It was at one of Fezziwig's parties that Scrooge had met his love, Belle.

Ignorance and Want

The Ghost of Christmas Present shows Scrooge the two children he calls Ignorance and Want. "They are Man's and they cling to me, appealing from their fathers. This boy is Ignorance and this girl is Want. Beware them both, and all of their degree, but most of all beware this boy for on his brow I see that written which is Doom, unless the writing be erased." These two children, described as "Yellow, meagre, ragged, scowling, wolfish" seem to represent the danger of poverty.

Dickens seems to suggest that Want (or need) is to be feared but that Ignorance is the worst trait as that can lead to Want. If people are educated, taught how to work and provide for their families and how to look out for one another (and overcome their current ignorance) then the cycle of poverty can be broken and avoided in the future (there will be no need for "want".) In short, he is making a point about education and saying if the poor remain uneducated then they cannot hope to improve their situations.

Belle

Dickens doesn't present female characters in very much detail in "A Christmas Carol." We meet Belle when Scrooge is transported back in time with the Ghost of Christmas Past.

Belle and Scrooge were in love until he started putting money before his relationship with her, "our contract is an old one. It was made when we were both poor and content to be so, until, in good season, we could improve our wordly fortune by our patient industry, You are changed. When it was made, you were another man." Even the use of the word "contract" makes it seem as if Scrooge is most interested in business. To be "poor and content" is not something that Scrooge is able to identify with until he sees the Cratchits enjoying a frugal Christmas, content with the company of one another. The reminder of his break up with Belle is almost too much for Scrooge and he begs the spirit, "Show me no more!" Later we learn that Belle married someone else and had a child with him whereas Scrooge remained alone.

The Ghosts

Jacob Marley

Jacob Marley was Scrooge's business partner before he died; he is the first ghost to appear to Scrooge. His name, like that of Ebenezer, has Biblical connotations.

At the start of the story, Dickens uses repetition to emphasise the fact that Marley has passed away. Within the first page he repeats this idea several times, "Marley was dead: to begin with," is followed by "Marley was as dead as a door-nail," then "Marley was as dead as a door-nail" again before "Scrooge knew he was dead? Of course he did!" Finally there is discussion of Marley's funeral and how Scrooge was the "sole mourner." These references are all within the first four paragraphs of the text! This repetition leaves the reader in no doubt that the first time we see Marley it is his ghost.

Scrooge first sees a vision of Marley when his face appears in place of the knocker on his front door. Although Scrooge dismisses the vision at the time, "Pooh-pooh" this does foreshadow the arrival of the ghost of Marley, later that evening. The theme of the supernatural is introduced and tension is built.

Whilst in business Marley and Scrooge cared only about their profits and took no responsibility for the effect they might be having on other people. Marley has now been dead for seven years and has clearly seen the error of his ways, "Mankind was my business; charity, money, mercy, forbearance, and benevolence, were, all, my business. The dealings of my trade were but a drop of water in the comprehensive ocean of my business!" He suggests that it is our character, our attitudes and actions towards others which give meaning to our lives. Our work and daily activities are but a "drop of water" in comparison to the meaningful parts of life such as our relationships with others. Our "business" can be seen as the requirement to love and care for other people.

As this ghost appears to Scrooge he is wrapped in chains which are made of "cash-boxes, keys, padlocks, ledgers, deeds, and heavy purses" which symbolise his greed during his life. Marley is now "doomed to wander through the world," suffering in the afterlife because of his uncaring, money-grabbing behaviour whilst he was alive. Marley's appearance serves as the first warning to Scrooge that he too could yet be punished for his attitude and lack of social responsibility if he fails to change his self-centred ways. Marley has realised "Mankind was my business" and he is helping to try and make Scrooge (and the reader) form the same conclusion, that Mankind is all of our business and we must all look after one another. Marley is condemned to an "incessant torture of remorse," clearly regretting his actions and destined to do so forever.

Scrooge is described as Marley's "sole friend," highlighting how lonely they were in pursuit of money. He was also, sadly, the "sole mourner" at Marley's funeral. The repetition of the word "sole" emphasises the solitary nature of their work and how Scrooge and Marley were concerned only with their own profits, not with their relationships with others.

Before he leaves, Marley helps with the structure of the story as it is he who tells Scrooge (and the reader) that he will be visited by three more spirits over the next three nights. This helps to guide the reader and assists them in following the plot of the novella.

Ultimately, Marley can be seen as the voice of Dickens as he is a character who has learned the lesson of social responsibility and has realised the need to look after your family, friends and employees during life so that you are not punished after death.

The Three Spirits

Unlike Jacob Marley, the other ghosts are not depictions of people who have died, instead they are incarnations of Christmas. They force Scrooge to reconnect with his past (including revisiting some painful memories) and show him how others are currently celebrating Christmas. Finally the Ghost of Christmas Past gives Scrooge an indication of what the future might be like if he continues to be driven only by money and live in ignorance of others around him.

The Ghost of Christmas Past

The appearance of the Ghost of Christmas Past appears to Scrooge in the form of both a child and an old man, "It was a strange figure – like a child: yet not so like a child as like an old man, viewed through some supernatural medium, which gave him the appearance of having receded from the view and being diminished to a child's proportions."

This ghost shows Scrooge his younger self so it is fitting that he adopts the appearance of both young and old (Scrooge's past and present). He wears "a tunic of the purest white and round its waist was bound a lustrous belt, the sheen of which was beautiful. It held a branch of fresh green holly" and glows like a candle. The white may symbolise the innocence and purity associated with childhood and the green holly gives the spirit a Christmas themed accessory!

Just before he leaves his light is extinguished by Scrooge, "he seized the extinguisher-cap, and by a sudden action pressed it down upon its head." It seems as if Scrooge has been able to ignore the painful memories of his childhood by blocking them out or "extinguishing" them, just as he does with this spirit who takes a form similar to a candle. However, Scrooge is unable to extinguish the light completely which suggests some of those memories and lessons he has learnt during his time with this ghost will remain with him.

The Ghost of Christmas Present

This spirit is a large, happy man, "there sat a jolly Giant, glorious to see, who bore a glowing torch, in shape not unlike Plenty's horn, and held it up, high up, to shed its light on Scrooge." Again we see the use of light, as if the spirit has come to literally and metaphorically "shed light" on Scrooge's misdemeanours before allowing him to realise he must change. He is "clothed in one simple green robe, or mantle, bordered with white fur," not looking unlike a traditional representation of Father Christmas.

This spirit shows Scrooge how others are celebrating Christmas. In many ways Scrooge has been blind to the celebrations and happiness around him. This ghost can be compared to that of Jacob Marley. Whereas Marley is now chained and miserable and forced to repent his sins for eternity, the Ghost of Christmas Present is happy and free which is even reflected in his physical appearance. The ghost wears flowing robes, has bare feet and his "dark brown curls were long and free; free as its genial face, its sparkling eye, its open hand, its cheery voice." The spirit aims to show Scrooge how others are experiencing Christmas: those who are celebrating and those who are suffering.

As if modelling good behaviour and social interaction, this ghost has a positive effect on others in the town, "he stood with Scrooge beside him in a baker's doorway, and taking off the covers as their bearers passed, sprinkled incense on their dinners from his torch." It is as if he is showing Scrooge that he must give to others, rather than being most concerned with the amount of money he can take from them. It is in that way that Scrooge can be similarly freed from his current worries and miserable nature.

The Ghost of Christmas Yet to Come

This spirit appears to be the most threatening. Scrooge is clearly afraid of him, "I fear you more than any spectre I have seen." This ghost looks somewhat like the Grim Reaper, "It was shrouded in a black garment, which concealed its head, its face, its form, and left nothing outstretched save one outstretched hand." Just as the Grim Reaper is said to collect people after they have died and so can be considered a personification of Death, so this character's aim is to warn Scrooge that he is facing a lonely demise and further torment if he does not start thinking of others and caring for those around him.

The fact he doesn't talk and only gestures with a bony finger makes him particularly intimidating; Dickens even refers to him as a "phantom." It is this ghost that finally ensures that Scrooge is set to change his ways as soon as he wakes up from his night of revelations. His lack of feeling and compassion for others has died and so in a way he needs to be re-born into a happier life.

Rather than trying to get rid of the ghost as quickly as possible as Scrooge did with the Ghost of Christmas Past, this time Scrooge seems reluctant to return to his own reality.

He is, however, determined to improve his relationships with others once he is released from the powers of this final spirit.

Check your understanding

Show your understanding by comparing the three spirits

Fill in the following grid to show your understanding of each of the ghosts which visit Scrooge after Jacob Marley:

Ghost of Christmas Past	Ghost of Christmas Present	Ghost of Christmas Yet to Come
Looks like..	Looks like..	Looks like..
Shows Scrooge..	Shows Scrooge..	Shows Scrooge..
What is the Ghosts personality like?	What is the Ghosts personality like?	What is the Ghosts personality like?
Scrooge Learns..	Scrooge Learns..	Scrooge Learns..
The Spirit leaves when..	The Spirit leaves when..	The Spirit leaves when..

Part 7

Key themes and techniques

Loneliness and isolation

The theme of loneliness is apparent from the start of the novella when Scrooge rejects the offer from Fred to spend Christmas with his family and instead returns to his cold house alone.

It does seem that Scrooge chooses his own isolation and so it is difficult to feel any sympathy for him and his situation during the opening section. He is completely preoccupied with making money and has no desire to look out for anyone but himself, "It's enough for a man to understand his own business, and not to interfere with other people's." It is clear that Scrooge has isolated himself; it is not that others have constantly pushed him away. Quite the contrary, Fred is determined to invite him to Christmas dinner every year, even if Scrooge does keep refusing, "I mean to give him the same chance every year, whether he likes it or not, for I pity him."

It is not until Scrooge meets the Ghost of Christmas Past who takes him back to his childhood and his days at school that we see a young and lonely Scrooge. "The school is not quite deserted…A solitary child, neglected by his friends, is left there still." We might expect Scrooge not to care, after all he has chosen a solitary life in adulthood but it is clear that this memory does affect him emotionally as, "he sobbed."

As the novella progresses Scrooge learns that it is love and companionship rather than money that brings people happiness. He enjoys parties he is shown by the ghosts and by the end is happy to join Fred for a family celebration.

Time

Time is handled in an interesting way by Dickens in "A Christmas Carol." The moving around from the present to the past, back to the present and into the future before returning to the present could be very confusing. Thankfully Jacob Marley's visit at the beginning of the novella makes the structure clear. The three spirits which follow Marley's appearance are not reincarnations of dead people, they are instead time travellers who enable Scrooge to be reminded of his past and warned about his possible future.

Scrooge is whisked from one scene to another by the spirits and the pace is also increased by the threat of Tiny Tim's death and, indeed, the death of Scrooge himself. It is apparent that if he doesn't change his ways very soon then Tiny Tim will die from his affliction and lack of nutrition and care, and Scrooge himself will die a miserable and lonely man. The clocks strike to emphasise how little time there is left for Scrooge to change although it is never stated exactly how far away those deaths could actually be. It might be that without this pressure there would be a danger of Scrooge forgetting the lessons from the night he was visited by the spirits and slip back into his old, selfish ways.

In order that Scrooge can return to Christmas Day time is again manipulated by Dickens. The spirits all visit Scrooge at 1am, he goes to sleep at 2am then wakes up at midnight again so time seems to somehow re-set itself. Without this, Scrooge would wake up after Christmas Day is over and be less able to put his new caring attitude into practice. Whereas Scrooge is initially concerned with time being linked to money (for example when he doesn't want to give Bob Cratchit Christmas Day off work) he learns that time with family and friends is what is most important for a happy life.

Pathetic Fallacy - The Significance of the Weather

Dickens uses pathetic fallacy in "A Christmas Carol" to help the reader to understand the change occurring in his protagonist, Ebenezer Scrooge.

At the start of "A Christmas Carol" the weather is cold and frosty and seems to mirror Scrooge's disposition. He appears as heartless and "cold" when he is reluctant to let Bob Cratchit have Christmas Day off, when he refuses the invitation to have Christmas dinner with his nephew Fred and when he is unwilling to donate any money to the poor. Even his appearance emphasises the literal and metaphorical coldness which surrounds him, "A frosty rime was on his head, and on his eyebrows, and his wiry chin. He carried his own low temperature always about with him…" This effect is repeated by Dickens which effectively adds emphasis to the comparison.

In the opening stave it is as if Scrooge himself doesn't even notice the weather, "No warmth could warm, no wintery weather could chill him." Dickens seems to suggest that Scrooge is numb to the weather the same way he is numb to the hardship of others.

When Scrooge leaves the office and returns home we hear how "the fog and frost so hung about the black old gateway of the house, that it seemed as if the Genius of the Weather sat in mournful meditation on the threshold." It is as if Nature itself is personified and is unhappy in the presence of the old miser.

Once he is inside, instead of a warm glow that we might have expected, Scrooge continues his miserly ways by limiting the amount of light he allows in his house at night, "darkness is cheap, and Scrooge liked it." He clearly puts money above anything else, including his own comfort. It seems he has done this for so many years that he has become hardened to this way of life.

By the end of the novella, even though it's less than 24 hours later in "real time," Scrooge is a transformed character and the descriptions of the weather have changed too, "There was nothing cheerful in the climate or the town, and yet there was an air of cheerfulness abroad."

Finally we hear of the, "Golden sunlight; Heavenly sky" as Scrooge appears as a changed man who is now able to appreciate the goodness in people and recognise that love and relationships with others are of more value than money.

The Narrator

Dickens uses an omniscient narrator in "A Christmas Carol." This means that the story is told from another character's point of view. Thanks to the narrator Dickens's views are made perfectly clear to the reader.

The narrator adopts a humorous tone and narrates the story of Scrooge in a way which is engaging and lively. Since Scrooge himself isn't narrating, we can gain insights into his character and feelings in an order which is controlled by Dickens. It may also seem a more honest approach; if Scrooge was telling us the story, his voice may be seen as unreliable as he may withhold information or thoughts. A reader is more likely to trust an omniscient narrator.

The narrator of "A Christmas Carol" is very critical of Scrooge, just as Dickens is critical of the hard hearted, rich businessmen that Scrooge represents, "a squeezing, wrenching, grasping, scraping, clutching, covetous old sinner!" The narrator even adopts a sarcastic tone at times, for example when he talks of Scrooge arranging Marley's funeral for an "undoubted bargain." We, the readers are influenced by Dickens's use of language and the voice of his omniscient narrator so we learn that Scrooge and all who are like him should change their ways for the good of society.

Use of dialogue

The dialogue used by characters reveals their attitudes and what they are thinking or feeling. At the beginning of the novella Scrooge is very dismissive when he talks to Fred, just repeating the phrase, "Good day!" to dismiss his nephew after he is invited for Christmas dinner. His brief exclamation of "Bah! Humbug!" is one of the most recognised expressions in the story.

In contrast to Scrooge, Fred's tone is always cheerful, even when his offer is rejected, "A merry Christmas, uncle!" Similarly, the Cratchits are positive even when times are hard… Tiny Tim's famous line is "God bless us, every one."

Belle's dialogue reveals a sadness when she explains how she feels about Scrooge, "Our contract is an old one. It was made when we were both poor and content to be so, until, in good season, we could improve our worldly fortune by our patient industry. You are changed. When it was made, you were another man."

The Ghost of Christmas Past asks many questions of Scrooge to try and involve him in the sights he is seeing and to get him to connect with his feelings, "Your lip is trembling," said the Ghost. "And what is that upon your cheek?"

The Ghost of Christmas Present is more inclined to engage in dialogue which focuses on Scrooge's changing attitude to the revelations, "Will you decide what men shall live, what men shall die? It may be, that in the sight of Heaven, you are more worthless and less fit to live than millions like this poor man's child."

The Ghost of Christmas Yet to Come doesn't engage in dialogue at all, instead he just points in the direction Scrooge should look to learn what will happen to him if he continues leading a miserable miserly life.

When writing about Dickens's use of dialogue do consider what is revealed about the characters' attitudes from the way they speak.

Check your understanding

Dickens's use of description

Dickens paints vivid pictures with his use of language throughout the novella. See if you can complete the table by finding examples of the techniques and explaining the possible effects on a reader:

Technique	Quote	Effect on Reader
Adjectives	"A wicked old screw."	
Simile		At the start of the novella, Scrooge is described in this way. Just as, when forced open, an oyster may contain a pearl, so Dickens suggested there may be something worthwhile to be found in Scrooge too.
Metaphore	"Golden sunlight; Heavenly sky"	
Symbolism		The chains which Marley is bound in are covered in these artefacts which symbolise Marley's greed when he was living,
	"crisp air laughed"	
	"It was cold, bleak, biting weather"	The weather at the start of the novella mirrors Scrooge's mood and his cold hearted attitude to others.

Techniques	Quote	Effect on Reader
Senses – sound		These sounds build tension before the arrival of Marley's ghost
Senses – touch	"Bear but a touch of my hand there," said the spirit, laying it upon his heart, "and you shall be upheld in more than this!"	
Senses – smell	"even that the blended scents of tea and coffee were so grateful to the nose"	
Senses – taste	"The compound of the jug being tasted, and considered perfect, apples and oranges were put upon the table"	
		The Ghost of Christmas Past is given an air of innocence and childhood with the use of the colour white. The green is a colour usually associated with Christmas.
Hyperbole	"Such a bustle ensued that that you might have thought a goose the rarest of all birds; a feathered phenomenon"	

Check the end of the book for some answers!

Part 8

Writing about the novella

Read the question several times and plan any essay before you begin writing. If you're in an exam remember that planning time has been built into the exam time. No examiner expects (or wants) you to pick up a pen the minute you are told you can turn over the paper!

Include references to context if this is relevant but try to avoid putting all of this information in your introduction, even though that might be tempting. Instead, try to weave comments about the context into your essay. For example, you might be talking about how Dickens refers to poverty at the start of the novel with the two gentlemen who ask Scrooge for money for the poor. This might be a good opportunity to include how, due to the Industrial Revolution, there were many poor people in Britain at the time who were forced to endure poor conditions in workhouses if they were unemployed but wanted financial support.

Don't forget to show your understanding of the form and structure of the text. Try to avoid "tagged on" comments like "it is a novella." Instead, try to explore the effect of the form. You could, for example, explain how the form of a novella allows for a greater level of detail and development of the main character than a traditional short story. You could examine the use of staves to divide up the text (see the chapters on the use of a novella and staves for further analysis). Similarly with the structure, try to explain the effect on the reader e.g. of the time travelling in the text.

When using quotations remember to keep them fairly short. Zoom in on words and phrases which Dickens has used for effect. For example you might want to analyse the use of similes and metaphors and explore the comparisons Dickens has chosen, e.g. in the beginning why is Scrooge described as "solitary as an oyster"? Remember to put quotation marks around the whole quote and copy it accurately including any capital letters, punctuation and so on.

Remember to always use the best possible vocabulary you can and check your work at the end so that you can correct any errors in spelling, punctuation and grammar. Best of luck!

Sample Essay 1

Explore the transformation of Ebenezer Scrooge in "A Christmas Carol."

Ebenezer Scrooge is the protagonist of the novella. We follow his journey from a miserable penny-pincher to a man who realises the error of his ways and transforms into a more caring and compassionate citizen.

Scrooge is a lonely character at the start of the novella. Dickens's use of language reflects this when outlining Scrooge's relationship with his former clerk Marley, "Scrooge was the sole executor, his sole administrator, his sole assign, his sole residuary legatee, his sole friend, and sole mourner." The repetition of the word "sole" adds emphasis to the solitary nature of the lives led by Marley and now Scrooge.

Dickens uses Scrooge to criticise the divide between those who have money and those who do not. At the start of the novella it is hard to sympathise with Scrooge in any way. Dickens sums him up as, "a squeezing, wrenching, grasping, scraping, clutching, covetous old sinner!" The collection of verbs here all have a similar effect; Scrooge is presented as a character whose intention is to grab every last penny he can from anyone he encounters. Words like "squeezing" and "scraping" suggest his task is difficult; he is seemingly pinching pennies from those who can afford it the least.

Dickens also uses figurative language to describe Scrooge at the start of the novella, he is "Hard and sharp as flint." This comparison leads the reader to believe that Scrooge has a hard exterior which could cause pain to others. Similarly, Scrooge is described as, "solitary as an oyster." This simile, unlike the first, does suggest that there may be more to be discovered where Scrooge is concerned. Just as, when forced open, an oyster may reveal a pearl, so Dickens suggests there may be something worthwhile to be found within Scrooge too. Just as a pearl can be made from a grain of sand, so Scrooge can be transformed from something seemingly worthless and irritating into someone worth admiring.

Scrooge's pointed nose, thin lips and red eyes also give him a harsh appearance. The colour red has connotations of danger whilst his lips and nose suggest he is an unfriendly, spiky character. There is also a literal and metaphorical coldness associated with the early descriptions of Scrooge, "A frosty rime was on his head, and on his eyebrows, and his wiry chin. He carried his own low temperature always about with him…" Dickens's use of language again emphasises Scrooge's cold-hearted nature and attitude towards others at the start of the novella.

All these physical descriptions appear accurate when we see Scrooge reject his nephew Fred's best wishes with a "Bah! Humbug!" He also refuses to give any money to the two gentleman who are collecting for the poor and is reluctant to give his clerk Bob Cratchit any time off for Christmas, "It's not convenient." Scrooge is almost animalistic when he begrudgingly grants Cratchit Christmas Day off work as he leaves the office "with a growl."

When faced with Marley's ghost we finally see a more vulnerable side to Scrooge. Having been startled by the morphing of his door knocker into Jacob Marley's face, Scrooge is already somewhat on edge. He tries to joke with Marley's ghost, "There's more of gravy than grave about you, whatever you are!" but he "tried to be smart; as a means of distracting his own attention, and keeping down his terror." He even implores the ghost to help him, despite having resisted opportunities to help others earlier in the day, "Speak comfort to me, Jacob." He has a taste of his own medicine when the ghost replies, "I have none to give." From early in the novella Dickens makes it clear that we reap what we sow in life and in order for people to care about us we must care for them and look out for them in return.

The Ghost of Christmas Past seems to care for Scrooge and Scrooge returns to an almost childlike state in his presence. As Scrooge is taken to other places by the ghosts that visit him after Marley, we take a similar stance as we, the readers, watch the scenes with him. When transported to his own past by holding hands with the Ghost of Christmas Past (as a parent would with a child) Scrooge recognises his school. The ghost explains that the school is not deserted, even though it is the Christmas holidays, "A solitary child, neglected by his friends, is left there still." At this Scrooge shows some emotion and cries. It is clear he is starting to realise that it is not only money which brings happiness. He remembers, "There was a dear boy singing a Christmas Carol at my door last night. I should like to have given him something; that's all." His transformation has begun.

Next, the Ghost of Christmas Past shows Scrooge another Christmas from his childhood. This time Scrooge's sister (Fred's mother) arrives as a child and shows a young Scrooge affection, "Dear, dear brother." This suggests that he did receive love from his family through his life and it was he that chose to reject it in favour of his business. Although Scrooge had been left at school in the past, in this scene he was welcomed home by Fan. Their father had sent her to get him and she explains, "Father is so much kinder than he used to be, that home's like Heaven!" Dickens's use of language here suggests people can change – Scrooge's father has softened and home and family should be valued.

Finally, the spirit takes Scrooge to the house of Fezziwig, to whom Ebenezer was apprenticed as a young man. A direct comparison can be drawn between Fezziwig's approach to Christmas as an employer and Scrooge's own approach when talking to Bob Cratchit on Christmas Eve. Unlike Scrooge, Fezziwig is very happy to give his employees time off, "No more work to-night." The comparison allows the reader to see that an alternative approach to business is possible; Scrooge could change his attitude and be more supportive as an employer.

Mrs. Fezziwig arrives, as do other guests and they have a party. Scrooge involves himself fully in the celebrations, "his heart and soul were in the scene, and with his former self…" He shows he can enjoy himself if he can just recapture that time in childhood when time with friends and family was important and to be enjoyed rather than avoided.

Scrooge again makes it clear he is reflecting on his recent behaviour towards Bob Cratchit, "I should like to be able to say a word or two to my clerk just now!" He is wanting to make amends for the way he has been treating his hardworking clerk.

Before this spirit leaves, Scrooge is taken to a scene involving himself and Belle, a young woman he was once engaged to. Belle is explaining how she believes Scrooge's love is now money rather than her, "You are changed." She leaves him and Scrooge struggles with the pain as he is forced to watch the scene unfold, "Show me no more!" Scrooge later learns that Belle has married someone else and had a daughter. They are all laughing and celebrating together, a clear vision of the joy which could have been his if he'd valued the relationship and looked after that rather than his monetary wealth. It is unclear even at the end of the novella if Scrooge is capable of sharing his life with someone else in the future.

When faced with the Ghost of Christmas Present we are reminded that Scrooge's attitude is changing, "I went forth last night on compulsion, and I learnt a lesson which is working now. To-night, if you have aught to teach me, let me profit by it." Scrooge is taken by the ghost and shown people celebrating Christmas, "There was nothing cheerful in the climate or the town, and yet there was an air of cheerfulness abroad." People are "jovial and full of glee", playing and shouting.

The spirit takes Scrooge to the house belonging to Bob Cratchit and his family. Scrooge sees Mrs. Cratchit and some of their children happily waiting for Bob to return home with his youngest, crippled son, Tiny Tim. Despite being poor Bob Cratchit has "his threadbare clothes darned and brushed up" so it is clear the family make the best of what they do have, rather than dwelling on what they lack. The Cratchit family are seen as Christian and thankful to God, despite their financial hardships. The family enjoy Christmas dinner together and they make a toast, during which Tim delivers the famous line, "God bless us every one."

Scrooge, realising the difficulties Tiny Tim is facing, implores the ghost to tell him of the future, "tell me if Tiny Tim will live." He genuinely seems to care about the little boy's fate, in contrast to his early comments about the poor and how if they die it would "decrease the surplus population." His attitude has certainly changed, "say he will be spared." The ghost is clear that Tim will not survive if the current situation remains unchanged and the Cratchits continue to struggle on very little income.

At this moment the attention turns back to the Cratchits as Bob names Scrooge "the Founder of the Feast" in a toast. The alliteration makes this title memorable. Mrs. Cratchit is more reluctant to praise Scrooge, "I'll drink his health for your sake and the Day's." Scrooge is forced to admit the effect his miserly ways are having on those who have done nothing but be loyal to him.

Next the Ghost of Christmas Present takes Scrooge to see his nephew Fred. They are talking about Scrooge and his rejection of Fred's offer to spend Christmas with them. Despite his constant ill-treatment, Fred remains loyal to Scrooge, seeming to feel some responsibility for his Uncle and showing determination and a desire to continue giving his Uncle a chance to change his ways, "I mean to give him the same chance every year, whether he likes it or not, for I pity him." Whereas Scrooge has been determined to protect his money at the expense of is relationships with others, so Fred is determined not to give up on his Uncle. Again Scrooge is made to watch festivities being enjoyed without him, "he begged like a boy to stay." There is hope for Scrooge's future as it is not too late for him to join his family and celebrate Christmas for the first time in many years.

It is at this point in the novella that Ignorance and Want appear. When asked if there is no refuge for these two children Scrooge is reminded by the spirit of his words about the disadvantaged in society, "Are there no prisons? Are there no workhouses?"

No sooner does the Ghost of Christmas Present disappear than the final spirit, the Ghost of Christmas Yet to Come takes his place. This ghost looks somewhat like the Grim Reaper, "It was shrouded in a black garment, which concealed its head, its face, its form, and left nothing outstretched save one outstretched hand." Just as the Grim Reaper is said to collect people after they have died, a personification of Death, so this character's aim is to warn Scrooge that he is facing a lonely death and further torment if he does not start thinking of others and caring for those around him.

Firstly, this spirit shows Scrooge people who are talking about a man's death, "It's likely to be a very cheap funeral, for upon my life I don't know of anybody to go to it." Initially he cannot work out which person has died. He is then taken to a group who are sorting through Scrooge's belongings. The group again talk about the dead man in a very negative way, "a wicked old screw." They have even stolen the blanket Scrooge was due to be buried in, in a similarly uncaring way to the way Scrooge acted towards other whilst he was alive, "They'd have wasted it if it hadn't been for me… Putting it on him to be buried in… somebody was fool enough to do it but I took it off again."

Scrooge does eventually realise that this is the aftermath of his own death that he's witnessing, "I see, I see. The case of this unhappy man might be my own." After visiting a family who are pleased Scrooge has died because it meant they might have some relief from their debts, and the Cratchits who are mourning the death of Tiny Tim, the spirit takes Scrooge to a churchyard. It is here that Scrooge reads his own name on a gravestone, "No, Spirit! Oh no, no!" The repetition in his speech and the few words he uses show the anguish he feels as he realises the future that lies in wait for him if he refuses to change his ways. He vows to "honour Christmas in my heart, and try to keep it all the year. I will live in the Past, the Present, and the Future. The Spirits of all Three shall strive within me. I will not shut out the lessons that they teach." At this point the ghost disappears and Scrooge is returned to bed, his lesson learned.

In the final section of the novel Scrooge has the opportunity to show that he is a changed man. Dickens's use of similes show the attitude of the new Scrooge, "I am as light as a feather, I am as happy as an angel, I am as merry as a school-boy…" Repetition is used to emphasise Scrooge's happiness, "it was a splendid laugh, a most illustrious laugh. The father of a long, long line of brilliant laughs!" The weather is also used to reflect Scrooge's change in character, "Golden sunlight; Heavenly sky." This is in contrast to the frost which surrounded him earlier in the novella.

After checking that he hasn't missed Christmas Day, Scrooge arranges for a big turkey to be sent to the Cratchits. He wishes others a "Merry Christmas" then goes to Fred's house for a "wonderful party, wonderful games" just as he had seen with the spirit. Already Scrooge is reaping the rewards of making an effort and being friendly to others.

At the office the next morning Scrooge gives Bob Cratchit a rise in wages. The final paragraphs of the novella confirm that Scrooge is indeed a changed man, "Scrooge was better than his word. He did it all and infinitely more." His journey is complete and we, the readers, are left with an understanding that people can change and society is a much better place if we all look out for one another.

Sample Essay 2

Discuss the ways in which Dickens presents wealth and poverty in "A Christmas Carol"

One of Dickens's aims when writing "A Christmas Carol" was to comment on the poverty of the 1840s and criticise the attitude of the rich towards the less wealthy. At the time many who were living in poverty ended up in workhouses and most did not or could not call upon charities or organisations for financial assistance. Dickens himself experienced poverty when his family went into debt when he was still a child, so it is unsurprising that he makes reference to this key theme in a number of his works, including "A Christmas Carol."

At the start of the novella Scrooge is seen as someone who is most concerned with making money and spending as little of it as possible. He refuses to give any money to the poor when given the chance on Christmas Eve. A new Poor Law had been introduced in Britain to try to combat the large numbers of poor people in the country at the time. It stated that in order to receive any financial assistance, anyone without a job was required to enter a workhouse if they wished to receive support with money and housing. There was a belief that poor people were lazy so workhouses were deliberately very difficult places to be. Despite this, when the visiting gentlemen ask Scrooge for money he replies heartlessly, "Are there no prisons?" He suggests that the poor be left to die to "decrease the surplus population." It is clear that Scrooge has much to learn about how poor people have families and work hard, so deserve to be respected and helped by those more fortunate than themselves.

Scrooge doesn't even allow himself the benefit of much light in his own home, "darkness is cheap, and Scrooge liked it." Scrooge, like many others in Britain during the Victorian era, seems to fear poverty above anything else. He lives in some discomfort just to save money.

When returned to his childhood and time as a young man by the Ghost of Christmas Past, Scrooge is reminded of why his relationship with Belle broke down. Belle explains how the pursuit of money has become Scrooge's priority, rather than his relationship with her, "our contract is an old one. It was made when we were both poor and content to be so, until, in good season, we could improve our wordly fortune by our patient industry, You are changed. When it was made, you were another man." Even her use of the word "contract" makes it seem as if Scrooge is most interested in business. To be "poor and content" is not something that Scrooge is able to identify with until he sees the Cratchits enjoying a frugal Christmas, content merely with the company of one another.

Scrooge pays his clerk Bob Cratchit very little, only fifteen shillings a week, and clearly expects long hours from him. He reluctantly grants him Christmas Day off after Cratchit explains politely that this is customary. Despite his poor treatment, when Scrooge is taken to Bob Cratchit's house by the Ghost of Christmas Present he sees the family making the most of what little money they have. Bob Cratchit has "his threadbare clothes darned and brushed up" and expresses his thanks to Scrooge for the little wages he does pay by naming him "Founder of the Feast." In the novella the poor characters such as the Cratchit family are presented by Dickens as good, hardworking and caring people whereas Scrooge himself seems to represent the selfish wealthy people in society. Despite his financial security Scrooge is miserly, greedy and self-centred, especially when we first meet him. Dickens is emphasising his belief that money doesn't necessarily bring happiness.

Fred, Scrooge's nephew and Fezziwig, his former employer act as role models to Scrooge during his night of revelations. They arguably represent the middle class who are more generous and keen to prioritise others rather than themselves, particularly at Christmas. Both throw parties for their family and friends; Fezziwig also includes his employees showing that businessmen don't have to be heartless and uncaring as Scrooge has been. Fred effectively acts as a contrast or "foil" to Scrooge, demonstrating that it is rewarding to spend money on Christmas festivities and it is possible to be successful and financially secure without being neglectful towards others.

Scrooge, at this point in the novella, is starting to care about others and seems genuinely concerned for the welfare of the Cratchits' youngest child, "tell me if Tiny Tim will live." His attitude is certainly altering, "say he will be spared." The Ghost of Christmas Present is clear that Tim will not survive if the current situation remains unchanged and the Cratchits continue to struggle on very little money. Money might not bring happiness but it does bring some physical security which Dickens suggests everyone should be entitled to.

Before the Ghost of Christmas Present leaves he introduces Scrooge to Ignorance and Want. These two children, described as "Yellow, meagre, ragged, scowling, wolfish", represent the danger of poverty and Scrooge is warned to "Beware them both." Dickens seems to suggest that Want (or need) is to be feared but that Ignorance is the worst trait as that can lead to Want. If people are educated and taught how to work and provide for their families and how to look out for one another (and overcome their current ignorance) then the cycle of poverty can be broken and avoided in the future - there will be no need for "want". Education is therefore presented by Dickens as a possible solution to the problem, an alternative to placing people living in poverty in horrid conditions in workhouses as had been suggested by the new Poor Law that had been introduced in Britain at the time.

The Ghost of Christmas Yet to Come shows Scrooge what would happen to him and his worldly possessions were he to die. Firstly this spirit shows Scrooge a group of people who are talking about a man's death, "It's likely to be a very cheap funeral, for upon my life I don't know of anybody to go to it." It is clear that Scrooge's money is now insignificant and he has to witness people talking of him in very negative ways; one describes him as, "A wicked old screw." One woman has even stolen the blanket Scrooge was due to be buried in, in a similarly uncaring way to the way Scrooge acted towards others whilst he was alive, "They'd have wasted it if it hadn't been for me… Putting it on him to be buried in… somebody was fool enough to do it but I took it off again."

Scrooge does eventually realise that this is the aftermath of his own death that he's witnessing, "I see, I see. The case of this unhappy man might be my own." After visiting a family who are pleased Scrooge has died because it meant they might have some relief from their debts the Ghost of Christmas Yet To Come takes Scrooge to see the Cratchits who are mourning the death of Tiny Tim. Scrooge is forced to realise that poverty can lead to death and can also drive people to disrespectfully steal from the dead. This shock, coupled with a visit to his own gravestone, is enough to finalise the change in Scrooge. He realises that poverty needs to be acknowledged and addressed.

In the final stave of the novella Scrooge arranges for a big turkey to be sent to the Cratchits, wishes others a "Merry Christmas" and then goes to Fred's house for a "wonderful party." Already Scrooge is helping others and reaping the rewards of making an effort and being friendly.

At the office the next morning Scrooge gives Bob Cratchit a rise in wages. The final paragraphs of the novella confirm that Scrooge is indeed a changed man, "Scrooge was better than his word. He did it all and infinitely more." His journey is complete and we, the readers, are left with the understanding that people can change and society is a better place if we all look out for one another.

Part 9

Check your understanding – The answers

Quick quiz based on the summary of the story:

1. Who was Scrooge's business partner who later visits him as a ghost?

   Jacob Marley

2. Who is Scrooge's clerk?

   Bob Cratchit

3. Before he returns home Scrooge declines two invitations, what are they?

   Fred's invitation to Christmas dinner and from two gentlemen who invite him to donate money to the poor.

4. Which inanimate object turns into the face of Jacob Marley?

   Scrooge's doorknocker.

5. Which sounds signal the arrival of Marley's ghost?

   Bells and chains.

6. Why is Marley being punished in the afterlife?

   For his poor behaviour towards others when he was alive and working as a loan shark with Scrooge.

7. Where does the Ghost of Christmas Past take Scrooge?

   Back to his school, to his memories of time with Fan, to Fezziwig's party when he was an apprentice and to his break-up with Belle.

8. What do we learn about Bob Cratchit's family Christmas, thanks to the Ghost of Christmas Present?

   They are poor with a crippled son (Tiny Tim) but they make the most of what they have and are thankful for it.

9. Which does the Ghost of Christmas Present tell Scrooge to fear the most: Ignorance or Want?

   Ignorance.

10. What is the Ghost of Christmas Yet to Come dressed in?

A long black cloak.

11. What is happening to Scrooge's belongings now that he's died?

    They're being sold.

12. What is the final sight that makes Scrooge determined to change his ways?

    He sees his own grave.

13. When the spirits have left and Scrooge is returned to the present, what does he send to the Cratchit family?

    A massive turkey.

14. Which invitations does he now accept that he refused at the start of the story?

    He attends dinner at Fred's house and donates to the poor.

15. What lesson has Scrooge learned by the end of the novella?

    That we must look after one another; our relationship with others are far more important than money.

Compare the characters of Scrooge and Fred.

Your answers might contain some or all of the following points:

Scrooge	Fred
Chooses isolation until the end of the novella.	Loves spending time with his family, partying and socialising with others.
Sees money as essential to a good life.	Sees family and love as essential to a good life.
Is likened to the cold both physically and in his demeanour.	Appears as a warm character both physically and in terms of his personality.
Hates Christmas (until the end).	Loves Christmas.
Is generally miserable.	Is generally happy and carefree.
Is determined as, until he meets the ghosts, he is sure that making money should be his only objective.	Is determined as he wont give up on Scrooge.

Show your understanding - comparing the three spirits

Your answers could contain some or all of the following points:

Ghost of Christmas Past	Ghost of Christmas Present	Ghost of Christmas Yet to Come
Looks like a mixture of young and old, is shaped like a candle.	A round jolly man not unlike our own Father Christmas.	Looks like the Grim Reaper as he wears a long black cloak with only a finger visible. He doesn't talk, just points.
Shows Scrooge painful memories of his childhood and early life.	Shows Scrooge how others currently celebrate Christmas including Fred and his family and the Cratchits.	Shows Scrooge what could happen if he doesn't change his ways – he could die a lonely old miser.
A calm and quiet ghost who seems to feel sorry for the childhood Scrooge has led.	It is quite jolly and happy until he meets Ignorance and Want as children to meet Scrooge.	Is the most serious of spirits, maintains a serious approach throughout his visit.
Scrooge struggles to engage with his past as it is presented to him.	Scrooge starts to show he is learning from the spirits.	Scrooge shows clearly that he has learned his lesson and is determined to change.
The Spirit leaves when Scrooge extinguishes the light.	Leaves when the4 bell chimes 12am and the next spirit appears.	Leaves when Scrooge offers a prayer that his current future should be changed.

Check your understanding - Use of description

Dickens paints vivid pictures with his use of language throughout the novella. See if you can complete the table by finding examples of the techniques and explaining the possible effects on a reader:

Technique	Quote	Effect on Reader
Adjectives	"A wicked old screw."	Scrooge is described in this way by the group discussing him after his supposed death. It is at this point that he realises how he will be remembered if he doesn't change his ways.
Simile	"solitary as on oyster"	At the start of the novella, Scrooge is described in this way. Just as, when forced open, an oyster may contain a pearl, so Dickens suggested there may be something worthwhile to be found in Scrooge too.
Metaphor	"Golden sunlight; Heavenly sky"	This description, found at the end of the story, shows how the atmosphere and mood has now changed and is to be treasured, just like gold and heaven.
Symbolism	"cash-boxes, keys, padlocks, ledgers, deeds, and heavy purses"	The chains which Marley is bound in are covered in these artefacts which symbolise Marley's greed when he was living,
Personification	"crisp air laughed"	Even the air during Christmas seems to be happy; Nature is personified.
Pathetic Fallacy	"It was cold, bleak, biting weather"	The weather at the start of the novella mirrors Scrooge's mood and his cold hearted attitude to others.

Techniques	Quote	Effect on Reader
Senses – sound	"a clanking noise, deep down below; as if some person were dragging a heavy chain"	These sounds build tension before the arrival of Marley's ghost
Senses – touch	"Bear but a touch of my hand there," said the spirit, laying it upon his heart, "and you shall be upheld in more than this!"	The Ghost of Christmas Past has control over Scrooge as he transports him back to his childhood.
Senses – smell	"even that the blended scents of tea and coffee were so grateful to the nose"	The descriptions of Christmas are particularly vivid and include sights and smells.
Senses – taste	"The compound of the jug being tasted, and considered perfect, apples and oranges were put upon the table"	The Cratchit family Christmas is described in detail using lots of different senses including taste.
Colours	"It wore a tunic of the purest white and round its waist was bound a lustrous belt, the sheen of which was beautiful. It held a branch of fresh green holly"	The Ghost of Christmas Past is given an air of innocence and childhood with the use of the colour white. The green is a colour usually associated with Christmas.
Hyperbole	"Such a bustle ensued that that you might have thought a goose the rarest of all birds; a feathered phenomenon"	The Cratchits really make the most of whatever they can afford so the goose is described as a "feathered phenomenom."

Part 10

Key Quotations

Learning quotations from the novella is important. Try highlighting those which you think you could remember after some revision. Drawing pictures to go with them, putting them on posters around your house or making flashcards out of them can help you to remember them.

Quote	Character(s) concerned and explanation
"Scrooge was the sole executor, his sole administrator, his sole assign, his sole residuary legatee, his sole friend, and sole mourner."	Scrooge, Marley The repetition of the word "sole" adds emphasis to the solitary nature of the lives led by Marley and now Scrooge.
"a squeezing, wrenching, grasping, scraping, clutching, covetous old sinner!"	Scrooge The collection of verbs here define Scrooge as a character whose intention is to grab every last penny he can from anyone he encounters.
"hard and sharp as flint,"	Scrooge A simile showing how Scrooge seems to have a hard exterior which could cause pain to others.
"solitary as an oyster."	Scrooge A simile suggesting that just as an oyster may contain a pearl, there may be something worthwhile to be found within Scrooge too.
"A frosty rime was on his head"	Scrooge Dickens's use of language again emphasises Scrooge's cold-hearted nature and attitude towards others.
"It's enough for a man to understand his own business, and not to interfere with other people's."	Scrooge Scrooge thinks people should just look out for themselves at the start of the novella.

"Are there no prisons?"	Scrooge When asked for a donation of money for the poor Scrooge comments that he thinks the poor should be put in prisons, workhouses or left to die.
"decrease the surplus population."	Scrooge Scrooge is happy for the poor to be left to die, showing his cold-heated attitude towards others.
"every idiot who goes about with 'Merry Christmas' on his lips, should be boiled in his own pudding…"	Scrooge Scrooge shows his contempt for Christmas whilst adding a touch of humour.
"Bah! Humbug!"	Scrooge Possibly the most famous expression in the text which shows Scrooge's rejection of anything to do with Christmas during the opening of the novella.
"He had so heated himself with rapid walking… his face was all in a glow."	Fred Fred emits both a physical and metaphorical warmth to those around him. He can be compared to the coldness of Scrooge at the start of the text.
"I mean to give him the same chance every year, whether he likes it or not, for I pity him."	Fred Fred refuses to give up on his Uncle at the start. Scrooge needn't be isolated as he has family who care for him.
"cash-boxes, keys, padlocks, ledgers, deeds, and heavy purses."	Marley, Scrooge Marley is bound in chains with these artifacts hanging from them. The purses and so on symbolise his greed during his life and act as a warming to Scrooge that he also will not be at peace when he dies if he continues to lead a life of selfishness and greed himself.
"It was a strange figure – like a child: yet not so like a child as like an old man."	Ghost of Christmas Past This ghost shows Scrooge his younger self so it is fitting that he adopts the appearance of both young and old.
"There was a dear boy singing a Christmas Carol at my door last night. I	The Ghost of Christmas Past The Ghost of Christmas Past starts to bring about a

should like to have given him something."	change in Scrooge as he begins to reflect on his recent behaviour towards others…
"No more work to-night."	Fezziwig Fezziwig shows how employees can be given time off so Scrooge could change his attitude and be more supportive as an employer.
"You are changed."	Belle, Scrooge Belle highlights that since they'd been together Scrooge had changed and become obsessed with money (to the point that he was more interested in that than in their failing relationship).
"there sat a jolly Giant… who bore a glowing torch."	Ghost of Christmas Present The light suggests the spirit has come to literally and metaphorically "shed light" on Scrooge's misdemeanours. The Ghost of Christmas Past also has a light which Scrooge extinguishes.
"*They were not a handsome family; they were not well dressed… But, they were happy.*"	Bob Cratchit Despite struggling for money, Bob is a reliable, loving and kind man who makes the best of his situation.
"It was shrouded in a black garment, which concealed its head, its face, its form, and left nothing outstretched save one outstretched hand."	The Ghost of Christmas Yet To Come This ghost looks like the Grim Reaper which is fitting since he shows Scrooge his future death.
"honour Christmas in my heart, and try to keep it all the year."	Scrooge By the end of the novella the change in Scrooge is complete.
"I will not shut out the lessons that they teach."	Scrooge Scrooge shows that he will remember the lessons the three spirits have taught him and will act on them in the future.
"I am as light as a feather, I am as happy as an angel,	Scrooge

I am as merry as a school-boy…"	More similes describe how Scrooge is a changed character by the end of the text. These can be compared to the similes used at the start to show the character's progression.
"God bless us, every one."	Tiny Tim Tiny Tim's expression is one of hope and positivity at the end of the novella.
"Golden sunlight; Heavenly sky."	Scrooge Scrooge is a changed man at the end of the text and the positivity is reflected in the use of colour and description. This can be compared to the cold frost at the start of the text.

Printed in Great Britain
by Amazon